A Guide

PRAYER

When Troubled

AFFIRMATION BOOKS
WHITINSVILLE, MASSACHUSETTS

A Guide

PRAYER

When Troubled

MARTIN C. HELLDORFER

Art: Richard Buccina
Käthe Kollwitz

Published with ecclessiastical permission

First Edition
© 1985 by Martin C. Helldorfer

Library of Congress Cataloging in Publication Data

Helldorfer, Martin C.
    Prayer, a guide when troubled.

    1. Prayer.   2. Meditations.   3. Consolation.
I. Title.
BV210.2.H415   1985   242'.4   85-13561
ISBN 0-89571-024-2

Printed by
Mercantile Printing Company, Worcester, Massachusetts
United States of America

*In memory of
John,
my father*

Acknowledgments

I gratefully acknowledge my indebtedness to those who knowingly and unknowingly shaped this book: Marie Kraus, Claire Brissette, James Leahy, Poppie Gadoury, Thomas Tyrrell, and Bernadette Casey.

Though presumptuous, I add the names of John Baptist de la Salle and Thomas Merton.

I thank Sister Anna Polcino, M.D., and Father Thomas Kane, Ph.D., D.P.S., whose wisdom and encouragement have been a support to so many, including myself.

Most importantly, I thank the residents and staff of the House of Affirmation at Hopedale, Massachusetts. The life that we share is, indeed, a most extraordinary gift.

Foreword

The signs of God's affirmation are everywhere: in creation, in relationship with Christ and his people, and in the sacraments, dogmas, and other elements of faith. There is really no limit to divine love, and these many signs draw us to respond in prayer where God's spirit is free to affirm us in a special way. Our prayer may take many forms; each one is a way to God.

This book is a gift from Brother Martin Helldorfer to all of us as a guide to the experience of prayer. It encourages us in faith.

Feast of the Ascension
16 May 1985

Thomas A. Kane, Ph.D., D.P.S.
Priest, Diocese of Worcester
Publisher, Affirmation Books
Boston, Massachusetts

Preface

The words that follow are written for those who are troubled. In this sense the book has been written for a few. Do you know the blackness of depression or the feeling that death is preferable to life? Do you understand how someone could associate sexuality with a guilt that can never be absolved? Or, do you know what it is like to be unloved? Could you pray at one time and now feel that you can pray no longer? Then these words are written for you.

While the book is written for a few, who is to say that those who are troubled are few in number? Isn't there a time when all of us are troubled? It is my hope that many will find these words helpful.

One person has written the text; many have authored it. They are the women and men residents of the House of Affirmation who have shared their life experience in so many differing ways. Their lives lie behind these words though no one person's experience is represented.

A word of caution. This book is a guide, but no solutions to specific problems nor answers to unsettling questions are given. The text is a guide insofar as the experience of many men and women lies behind the printed word. It is a guide in another way: this book will leave readers with a sense of how they can help themselves. See if this isn't the case for you. After you read the book, don't give it away. If it has helped you, keep it on your bookshelf for another day when reading it may again be helpful.

Easter Monday
8 May 1985

Martin C. Helldorfer
Hopedale, Massachusetts

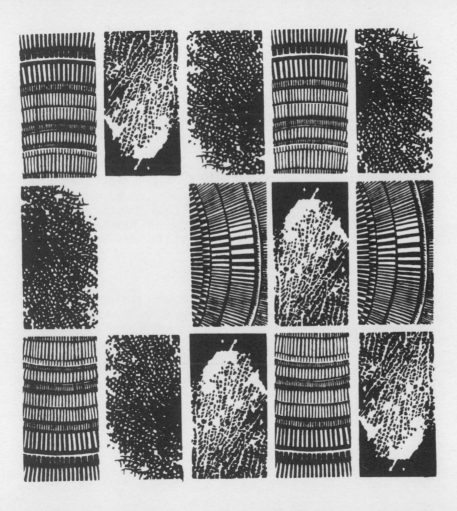

ord,

Open our eyes to see your hand at work in the splendor of creation and in the beauty of human life.

Touched by your hand our world is holy. Help us to cherish the gifts that surround us, to share your blessings with our brothers and sisters, and to experience the joy of life in your presence.

Prayer, Seventeenth Sunday of Ordinary Time

If you pick up a book . . .

*and simply read it through, you are wasting your time.
As soon as any thought stimulates your mind or your
heart . . . put the book down because your meditation has
begun. To think that you are somehow obliged to follow
the author of the book to his own particular conclusion
would be a great mistake. It may happen that his
conclusion does not apply to you. God may . . . have
planned to give you quite a different grace than the one
the author suggests you might be needing.*

Then Jesus went with them to a place called Gethsemane, and he said to his disciples,

"Sit here, while I go yonder and pray."

And taking with him Peter and the two sons of Zebedee, he began to be sorrowful and troubled. Then he said to them,

"My soul is very sorrowful, even to death; remain here, and watch with me."

And going a little farther he fell on his face and prayed.

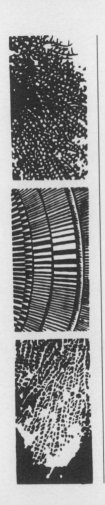

I.

*P*rayer is a movement toward intimacy. It cannot be forced. Time is needed for it to develop and its price is costly. A lifetime of shared joys and sorrows is involved. To force prayer is as ineffective as efforts to force intimacy. Prayer, like intimacy, is an almost unrecognizable and wordless realization of what has come to be.

Phrased another way, prayer is the posture of someone who at all times and in every place knows that everything is from God.

Prayer
is
also
a
word
we
use
to
describe
a
relationship.

It
is
a
word
to
speak
of
the
bond
between
God
and
ourselves.

It
is
a
bond
likened
to
the
love
between
mother
and
child—

unbreakable,
but
hardly
untroubled.

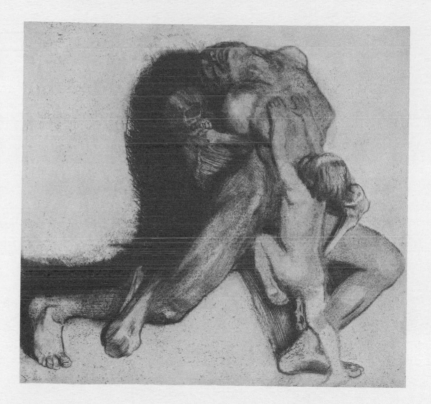

The language of prayer is that of love. To ask how to pray is like asking how to love. We start with words but end in silence.

When we grow in love, especially romantic love, we want to voice that love time and again. But words are not enough. Silence is needed. A man grew to love a woman. Without being aware of his nervousness, he frequently assured her of his love. One day he noticed a pleading in her eyes. "Hold me," she said, and from that moment he knew that there is a time to be wordless. Why solitary prayer? Because there is a time for it.

The silence of love is a place of rest. Think of prayer as such a place.

God has spoken to us in the person of Jesus. He was remarkably silent in the midst of his life. We are God's continued revelation. Our lives are a prayer. They are a way of voicing something that our lips cannot utter. We try to find words but must be content with silence. The more we sense the sacredness of what we are about, the quieter we become. The prayerful person is silent yet worldly.

When lives are shared there is a time for words. But to reduce a relationship to words is a mistake. To reduce prayer to words is equally unfortunate.

Much of life is lived in silence; all of life evokes it.

When language ceases, silence begins. But it does not begin because language ceases. The absence of language simply makes the presence of Silence more apparent.

Prayer involves learning to rest.

Again, think of prayer as a word we use to describe our relationship with God. We are always in relationship; we are always praying. Quietness is needed to recognize prayer.

We can walk a dozen times along a familiar path and never notice its beauty. Stop for a moment; sit down and rest; look closely. The world breaks open. We see what was unseen. The more contemplative we become, the more we notice. These are the moments when we have a hint of the Life behind our life. But the world seldom opens without a moment of rest. Once it yields, memory of those moments lingers.

When the world of nature opens before us we marvel at its beauty. We do well to turn our eyes toward ourselves. We, too, are God's creation, God's work of art. Often we live as if we were our own. Failing to make ourselves into the persons we are not, we become painfully aware of the gap between what we want to become and what we are. No wonder we are restless.

The fact is that we are God's work of art, wholly and uniquely so. Suppose we awakend to that truth? Then our stance toward ourselves would be altered in a remarkable way. If the person beside us is also God's work of art, what a difference that would make. We need to quietly accept the fact that we are formed preciously. That truth transforms. It is difficult to run through art-filled places. In the moment of silence, how much falls away and how effortlessly what remains falls into place.

We have to help one another find moments of rest. Sometimes we fear quiet because we fear boredom. We turn on a stereo for background music. We assure ourselves that it does not interfere with our concentration. Sometimes we say that after a time we hardly hear the radio.

When something that is present is not heard we are saying that the uttered word no longer touches us. We might say, perhaps too harshly, that we have become impervious to what has broken into the world. We have deadened ourselves to the extent that the word no longer matters.

We deaden our lives when we forget that they are rooted in silence. Silence is the place from which to hear. If we do not hear, we cannot respond.

Think of what would happen to our speech if there were no pauses between our words. It would become senseless. Communication would falter. Without moments of silence our activity loses its value.

Outward quiet is difficult to find; inward silence is even more elusive. Many times we live so alienated from our own inwardness that when we find a moment of silence we think of It as prayer. Once quieted we then move apart from prayer at the moment when we are ready for it.

Silence is the ground of human involvement, be it work or play. That is why we need to help one another become inwardly quiet. When quieted we are invited to become attentive to the beauty and goodness of life. We will also see its violence and injustice. Before long, persons of prayer are led back to the marketplace where their presence is so necessary.

There is more silence than language in love.

It is . . . in silence that we should seek the native soil in which faith can grow. . . .

Between that unheard of happening, the Incarnation, and the being of man, silence interposes itself as a kind of buffer. . . .

Thus, in approaching God, we approach the silence with which God himself is surrounded.

We put frames of words around silence and shells of stone and wood around emptiness, but it is the silence . . . that finally matters and out of which the Gospel comes as word.

II.

We associate the words peace and tranquility with prayer. And rightly so. Yet for many of us, prayer is not a comforting experience; it is one of emptiness. Like the poet, we feel that there is no face on which our gaze can rest; there is only endless desert. When we feel this way, nothing is wrong. The climate of prayer is often, if not usually, the desert.

Deserts are not distant places. They are within cities and as close as our hearts. They are places of space created by absence. When loved ones move away, the desert is terrible. Consider friendship or marriage. When two persons pledge their love they feel as if they know one another. However, when they begin to change, especially when one changes at a pace different from the other, the relationship is troubled. The moment they recognize that what has been cannot be recovered and that a new relationship must be found between them, they begin to awaken to the realization that they have promised fidelity, not constancy. However, before that discovery is made, the two must live in a moment of suspension when they feel as if they have lost each other. That is a desert.

Something similar happens in prayer. When we change, our relationship to God changes. We seemingly withdraw from one another. Since we are always changing, God is always being lost.

We begin therapy. If successful, that is, if we change, God will surely be lost. Our employment affects what we see and value. Change it, and our prayer is affected. Schooling does the same. So does romantic love. Every life experience touches our relationship to God.

Haven't we lost God before? Look back over life.

A child of seven prays beside his bed for his parents. His trust is appealing and his simplicity disarming.

A youngster of twelve has his God beside him as companion and helper. We smile.

As an adolescent, that same person may reject the God of his younger years. His God is absent.

That same fellow may find God as a young adult.

And so it goes.

Each change creates a gap. When we look backward in
time it is relatively easy to admit to the way that God is
lost and found. It is immensely more difficult to
acknowledge the same changes in adult life. However, no
one escapes such moments.

To arrive where you are, to get from where you are not,
    You must go by a way wherein there is not ecstasy.

In order to arrive at what you do not know
    You must go by a way which is the way of ignorance.

In order to possess what you do not possess
    You must go by the way of dispossession.

In order to arrive at what you are not
    You must go through the way in which you are not.

For some, the gap is extended. When this occurs we live in a desert. That is unsettling.

For others, the moment of suspension is an instant. Change is not troubling for them. The new intermingles with the old in a way that smooths transitions.

If life experience is drawn as a line, a few could depict their lives as relatively continuous. They are the persons for whom change is not particularly troubling. They are molded slowly by everyday life:

Others know desert experiences now and again. At times there are periods when they are settled. Their life experience might be drawn this way:

Still others know what it is to have one major life crisis that seems to divide their lives into halves. They speak of a before and after of one never-to-be-forgotten troubling time:

And some know the feelings of living in a near continuous desert where tranquil moments are as rare as the moments of crisis are for others. They live within the gaps:

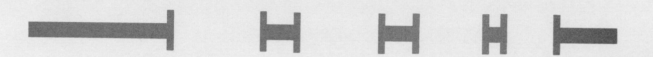

When in crisis, when something or someone is lost, there is seldom an awareness and certainly no assurance that the moment will pass. We are suspended. That is what is so unsettling. It feels as if there is no end:

Some paths may be easier; no one way is better.

There is a waiting
which is desire.

There is a silence full of sound.

There is a patience, wide as a world
aburst with strength . . .

There is a waiting
which is a growing,
a waiting with the swell and fall of breathing. . . .

There is a waiting . . .
like a womb heavy with child. . . .

There is a waiting like a wake,
the flicker of a solitary star
the only light, the candle,
a wavering sign,
an uncertain token. . . .

There is a waiting
chilling my bones. . . .

There is a waiting loud like a universe
far gone in gestation.

There is a loneliness
tight with terror,
ready to break adrift,
to roam the dark alluring sea.

But standing by the cross of Jesus were his mother, and his mother's sister, Mary the wife of Clopas, and Mary Magdalene.

The desert is a time when words falter.

The Eucharist is called the sacrament of the Real Presence. We need a theology of the Real Absence.

God's absence is a gift, however unwelcome. It is a hint of change, an indication of growth, and a path toward depth. There is no movement without crisis nor depth without loss. Nevertheless we often think that something is wrong when we feel as we do. We say to ourselves: what good is suffering? Of what value is emptiness?

Augustine wrote that Jesus departed from the sight of his followers so that they might find him in their hearts. The absence of God is the invitation to another discovery, not only in our hearts but in our involvement as well.

To glimpse the value of suffering, recall those to whom we turn when in need. Do we look for those who have been protected from suffering? On the contrary, we search for persons who have known it. If there is a crisis today, it is that we protect one another from change. The cost is depth. What home, parsonage, rectory, or community creates a space for those who struggle with disbelief? When is there time for emptiness in the Church's ministers? Yet without crisis moments there is no depth. No wonder we turn less and less frequently to the Churches for understanding. Behind those walls are the overly protected. No, there is little need to worry when we struggle with prayer. The time for concern is when we are pious. Remember: love is faithful, not necessarily constant.

III.

*C*an we help ourselves when unable to pray?

Yes.

We can stop praying.
Better still, we can stop trying to pray.

When one way of praying has died, why repeat that way
so doggedly? Why not move in another direction? If a
door is locked, why not try a window? If we seem
trapped, why not sit for a moment and look about? What
have we to lose?

One of the problems with prayer is that it is sometimes a relationship that we construct. Without knowing it, we build a prayer life that serves any number of functions, often protective ones. To let go of that approach is threatening. Yet, if God is truly lost, certainly our decision to stop praying cannot make things worse. It is not prayer that we find difficult to relinquish; it is our need to control.

Recall the Scriptures. Isn't it God's faithfulness on which we rely? If we let go of prayer, will God let go of us? Hardly. To think otherwise is to lose perspective. Our relationship with God rests on love, not equality. In the desert we need trust more than effort. Discipline is for the city, surrender for the desert.

Instead of fretting, place the Scriptures beside an easy chair. Let them rest there. Their presence will be a sign of our desire as well as our inability to pray. Someday when we are less restless we may turn to them in a way that we would turn to any cherished words. But for now let them rest.

We can also learn to wait.

That, too, is difficult. We will return to prayer sometime but when and where that will be remains unknown. There is very little need to be anxious about that moment. We are held by God even when we flounder. Waiting is an act of faith, not rebellion.

Today is the first day of spring. I've waited for this day and have yearned for its warmth. But it snowed yesterday and this first day of spring is as wet and cold as any day of winter. I've been feeling down all day and I spent most of the morning complaining about the weather.

There is something humorous in the way that I live. I seem to endure the present moment by anticipating a future one and when the future arrives I destroy it by feeling that it is other than it should be. My attitude that the present is not-as-it-should-be robs the moment of some of its simplest joys and sorrows. This may be one of the reasons why I have such a difficult time trying to pray. After figuring out what prayer should be, I then end up berating myself that it is not as it should be or else I try to muster the will power to make it the way it ought to be. What a funny person I am. I think that I need a lot more snowy days in spring.

All of us do.

In the moment of waiting, listen: new life stirs.

To discover that life is not easy. Stern inward voices may keep us from relaxing. "Hurry," they say, "do something. Try harder. You are on dangerous ground. Something is wrong. Strengthen your back, tighten your muscles, awaken your will, and join your hands." Many people do. There is no need for that kind of violence. Stern voices need to be acknowledged, not followed. What we do need is sensitivity to less strident voices from quieter places.

Growth cannot be rushed. Timing is involved. A wisdom saying advises us to wait with open hands beneath ripening fruit. The wise person will know the moment to reach. It will correspond to the moment that the fruit falls. That is what waiting is all about. It is knowing the moment of readiness.

It is not what we believe about God that is so important; it is what God knows of us that is so valuable.

We can do something else when unable to pray. We can
let go of our preoccupation with what has died and look
in the direction of what is living. Follow that path.

When we focus on what is lively, we open ourselves to
discover the prayer that is already present but unseen.
Discipline, fasting, vigils, and the seemingly dark places
of asceticism are valuable but they are not the only way
to God. In fact, they are often distorted ones. Everyday
life with its pleasures and pain, beauty and ugliness, is
rich soil for prayer. Look for God in its shadows.

We live in one world, known to be two. The same reality that is profane at one moment is sacred at another. This world and another world, the profane and the sacred, are neither opposites nor identical. Moments of explicit prayer are times when the two worlds merge. That is why prayer is silent; we are held in two worlds where there is no possibility of speech—only a self-forgetful, wordless, resting Presence.

Instead of saying prayers, be still long enough to hear the quieting note of God's silent presence.

We can help ourselves inestimably each day by going in search of something beautiful. When found, do not take it home; let it stay where found. At first we may notice roses. Soon we will find beautiful things in the most unlikely places.

And lastly, pray by doing.

When unable to pray, let everything—work included—be a prayer. Forget about holy words and pious feelings. Become worldly. Invest in the work at hand. Is it a job? Work well. Is it conversation? Be attentive. Is it a book? Enjoy it. A meal? Relish it. This is not pretense; it is another act of faith.

There is a time when a kiss expresses love. To imagine that a kiss is the only way to show love is unfortunate. The moment of prayer is a particular way to express love. It is not the only way. We can love God and never know a moment of untroubled prayer. A relationship of love is not formed by a momentary act but in the life that surrounds it. In every relationship we have to look for ways to express love. No single act is privileged. When unable to pray with words and sentiment, move toward the world of involvement.

Again stern voices will be heard. "Don't you know the error involved in believing that work is prayer?" "Haven't you ever heard of the parent who shows love by doing only? Isn't that enough to warn you against making work into prayer?"

Those thoughts are a warning but not a deterrent. There is a sacredness in the workplace. Activity expressses love. Doing may not be everything when we are speaking of love, but it is something.

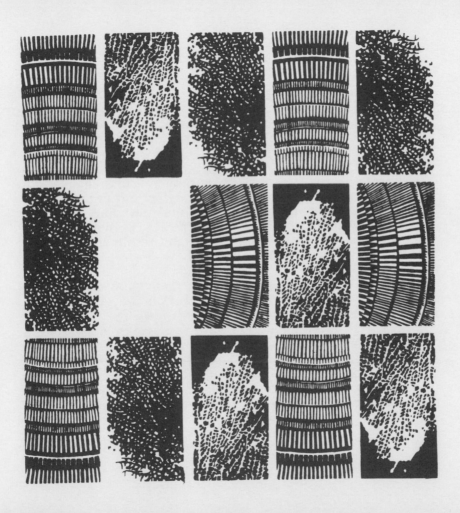

IV.

Someday, sometime, there may come a moment
when we are inclined to pray in a formal way. That desire
is a gift. No, it is not an invitation to an unusual nor to a
more intimate relationship with God. Rather, it is an
invitation to become aware of a relationship of love that
is already present. Everyday awareness is sleepy. When
we move into a moment of prayer, it is as if the
threshold that separates the known from the unknown is
lowered. We awake for a time.

There is no need to take formal time for prayer. No one will suffer if we do not. No one will be punished. Efforts to pray that rise from guilt reflect good will but they are not the fertile soil for intimacy. Again, someday, sometime, there may come a moment when we are inclined to pray. When that moment comes, we are well advised to listen.

Here, too, we need gentleness toward ourselves. If we do not listen we need not fear the consequences. There are those who say that if we do not respond to the invitation when given, it will be withdrawn. Do not believe them. If something is about to come into awareness, it is not easy to stop its emergence. Love is faithful as well as haunting.

When the moment to pray comes we will know what to do. Prayer is an art of sorts, a moment of self-forgetfulness when every stirring within the soul is drawn before God.

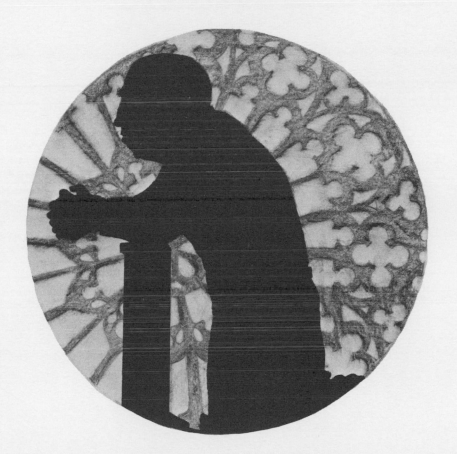

Some will say responding to the moment is easy—all that is required is to lift one's mind and heart to God. It is true that such a gesture is all that is needed but it is far from easy. Surrender is involved. Ask anyone who has shed a shell of piety, rebellion, or disbelief if you want to know how difficult it is to surrender. When all we have known is the desert, we develop protective shells. To pray involves such simplicity that most of us stand wary. However, once the shells are worn thin or even break—if only for an instant—we are inevitably pulled to find time for prayer. Memory of a glimpse is all that is needed.

Some will find time for prayer in the morning. A kiss upon waking is expressive of a whole way of living in relationship. Words at such a time are unnecessary and can even clutter the sentiment that is expressed. An extended and profound bow before God upon waking is an unfathomably rich prayer. Because we are remembering persons, the kiss and the bow linger throughout the day. Perhaps that is why there is morning prayer.

We move into prayer when the God about whom we are thinking becomes the person with whom we are present.

Some will find time for prayer in the evening. At nightfall
we have the day behind and the night before us. Prayer
at that time is as different from prayer in the morning as
sentiments at sunset differ from those at sunrise. There
is no need to praise one time over the other. The heart
knows a time for both.

Prayer involves not only the mind and heart, but body as well. We are wholly bodily persons; not only, but wholly so. Look at a discus thrower poised and ready to throw. A glance is enough to know what he is about. If a woman is bent over a desk with a book in front of her and if her fingers are embedded in disheveled hair, we surmise that she is studying. Such persons can deceive us. The discus thrower could be searching the ground for something lost and the woman at her desk might be sleeping. The possibility of deceiving ourselves or others is not the point. The fact is that our bodily presence speaks to what we are about. If we want to throw a discus we have to look like discus throwers. Human action, including prayer, entails expressing ourselves in bodily ways that reflect what we are about.

Becoming expressive is not easy. Again, it is a question of surrender. As soon as we express ourselves we are exposed. We are forced, as it were, from our inwardness. Once exposed, commitment follows. Lovers know this. What lovers want to stay in their minds? When love is reduced to mindfulness it soon ends. The challenge is to live in such a way that the inward and outward harmonize. No wonder we are inclined to make prayer into an inward affair. That grants freedom, or at least the look of freedom. It also breeds isolation. When inclined to pray we need to remember to lift our arms, bow our heads, drop to our knees, or find some way to manifest what stirs within. This is just as hard to do as to surrender to the fact that we are loved. Sometimes it takes years.

For every minute of prayer, spend two reflecting on life apart from prayer.

Awareness of ourselves as bodily persons may help us avoid some of the distortions that rise when we try to develop a prayer life. For instance, centuries of talk about prayer have made it into an esoteric activity. There are rules galore about what we should or should not do with our bodies. There is talk of how to breathe, eat, and control the senses. Some tell us of the necessity to relax each part of our bodies progressively. Others advise us of the need to empty our minds. As helpful as these suggestions are at times, they often enough mold us into religious artifacts rather than loving persons.

When with a loved one, do we try to empty ourselves of all thoughts? Do we need to control our attention when we embrace someone? Hardly. The more we are expressive, the more we recognize that we are wholly bodily persons. As this awareness awakens, the need to control ourselves is lessened. If we let ourselves become expressive during prayer, prayer becomes easier.

Most importantly, formal prayer has a rhythm all its own. Foremen have schedules; lovers do not. The pattern of prayer changes from day to day and year to year. There is no guarantee that our rhythm will be daily. Maybe it is weekly with Saturdays and Sundays as times of formal prayer. Maybe it is yearly when the summer brings its gifts. Some look back on their lives and recognize the rhythm in terms of years. No one pattern is better than another. The challenge is to respect the changing rhythms of our own lives. That involves remaining quiet enough to hear God's stirrings at any moment. When we try to mold ourselves into persons we are not, we may develop the look of virtue but we will have to live with the consequences of being unfaithful to ourselves.

And lastly, when the moment to pray comes, pray in that place. There is no need to find a special one. All places are sacred. Each house and room, every forest and city is holy. Some places, such as churches or the ground where a loved one is buried, are especially sacred. Even so, there is no need to choose those places to pray. We are in a sacred place when the moment comes.

Prayer is no guarantee that we will feel peaceful. When we pray God's light shines upon us. That light can leave us agitated as well as peaceful.

If prayer leads us toward increased flexibility, openness, and responsibility, we have a hint that our efforts to pray are informed. If we find ourselves increasingly isolated from others, we've a hint that our efforts are misdirected.

Prayer has to do with a way of living. It is not one activity beside so many others.

Often we fail to take time to pray because we have the haunting fear that something will be asked of us if we pray. That fear is well founded.

To stand wordlessly, quietly, and at times darkly before God day after day changes the way we touch the earth as well as others.

We need to remember that this world is God's world. Pope John XXIII thought of it as a garden rather than a museum. Most of us think of it as raw material. What a change takes place when we start to realize that our home is God's home.

V.

In bygone years, knights of the Round Table left on horseback to travel through dark forests in search of the Holy Cup. Each had to find his own path. That story is everyone's story before God. Today the horses, goblets, and kings are gone but the forest remains. The way is still pathless.

Are there guides? Certainly, but be cautious. The Masters urge us to pose a question to the guides we consider. Ask them what to do to keep unholy thoughts from disturbing us. If advised, you will know that the guide belongs to those who are of no account.

God speaks through every person, each happening, and all things. Yet no one speaks for God; neither Church, State, neighbor, nor loved one. We are always and everywhere alone before God. Sometimes it seems as if our only guide is our restlessness.

We are all wayfarers, persons journeying on roads never before taken. Another can help us to pray by journeying with us. However, alone or with another, the road remains unfamiliar. Beware of the person who speaks of knowing the path. Beware, too, of those who say that there are no guides and that we are always and everywhere isolated from one another. Being alone is not the same as being isolated. Travel with others. Trust those who are content to share the journey, yet do not expect them to walk an identical path. The journey is solitary. All ways of prayer, even proven ones, are mistaken insofar as they are not our own.

Try not to forget

—that God is both hidden and manifest, distant and
near. None of us knows God; all of us do.

—that a person of prayer is someone who discovers time
and again what the Hebrews of old knew so well—that we
unknowingly create idols. An idol is something that is
instead of.

—that God hides in pseudonyms. Our efforts to pray
falter if for no other reason than the god for whom we
search is not God. If we desire to pray we must live
among shadows in a world that is sacred but that we
find commonplace.

—that our movement toward God is lifelong. Every
balance once achieved is cast in doubt by changing
times and situations. Our need for conversion is never-
ending. Every decision opens another world that entails
still another surrender. Each turning toward God is a
partial one.

—that the unsettling reality of prayer is that in either ecstasy or depression there is never the surety that it is God who is there. Therein lies the incomprehensible significance of faith.

—that any conception of God is inadequate. Any understanding of prayer is limited. To say we know God or that we have experienced God is to walk on dangerous ground. The young speak that way. At the same time it is foolhardy to say that we do not know God or that we have never experienced God. Wisdom has a quietness about it.

—that to be faced by the inescapable, metallically cold and biting truth of our near constant self-seeking is to be cleansed by a fire that promises, at least as a hope, that at some moment we will be silent and let God work and speak.

Thoughts about prayer can leave us feeling lonely and frightened. However, remember that the person beside us likely feels the same way. If we realize that, we will feel less fearful and more connected to others. Reach out to them in caring and understanding ways.

Notes

Page 12 Richard Buccina, 1984.

Page 13 Prayer, Roman Missal, Seventeenth Sunday of Ordinary Time.

Page 14 Thomas Merton, *New Seeds of Contemplation* (New York: New Directions, 1961), p. 215.

Page 15 Scripture quotations are from *The New Testament* (Grand Rapids, Michigan: Zondervan Publishers, 1971), Matthew 26: 36-40.
Richard Buccina, 1984.

Page 18 Käthe Kollwitz, from: *Prints and Drawings of Käthe Kollwitz* (New York: Dover Publications, 1951), "Mother with Child in Arms," #27.

Page 19 Ibid., "Woman and Death," #23.

Page 22 Max Picard, *The World of Silence* (Chicago: Gateway, 1964), p. xix.

Page 23 Richard Buccina, 1984.

Page 28 Richard Buccina, 1984.

Page 31 Picard, *World of Silence,* p. 84.
Gabriel Marcel, *Introduction to The World of Silence,* p. xiv.
Frederick Buechner, *Telling the Truth* (New York: Harper and Row, 1977), p. 26.

Page 35 Richard Buccina, 1984.

Page 38 T. S. Eliot, *Four Quartets* (New York: Harcourt, Brace, and World (Harvest), 1943), p. 29.

Page 45 Jacques Theuws, *Transcendental Meditations* (Windsor, Ontario: The Netherlandic Press, 1982), pp. 49, 51.

Page 46 Richard Buccina, 1984.
         The New Testament, John 19:25.

Page 48 Richard Buccina, 1984.

Page 53 Richard Buccina, 1984.

Page 54 Anonymous.

Page 63 Käthe Kollwitz, "Woman Welcoming Death," #67.

Page 65 Richard Buccina, 1984.

Page 67 Richard Buccina, 1984.

Page 68 Richard Buccina, 1984.

Page 82 Richard Buccina, 1984.